PIANO . VOCAL . GUITAR

ELVIS
THE 25TH ANNIVERSARY CONCERT
LIVES

ISBN 978-1-4234-4577-7

Elvis and Elvis Presley are registered trademarks of Elvis Presley Enterprises, Inc., Copyright © 2009.
www.elvis.com

CORPORATION
7777 W. BLUEMOUND RD. P.O. BOX 13819 MILWAUKEE, WI 53213

Visit Hal Leonard Online at
www.halleonard.com

C.C. RIDER

Adapted and Arranged by
ELVIS PRESLEY

BURNING LOVE

Words and Music by
DENNIS LINDE

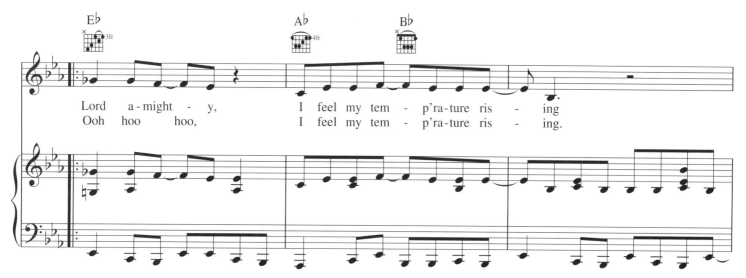

Lord a-might-y, I feel my tem-p'ra-ture ris - ing
Ooh hoo hoo, I feel my tem-p'ra-ture ris - ing.

WELCOME TO MY WORLD

Words and Music by RAY WINKLER
and JOHN HATHCOCK

I CAN'T STOP LOVING YOU

Words and Music by
DON GIBSON

STEAMROLLER
(Steamroller Blues)

Words and Music by
JAMES TAYLOR

YOU GAVE ME A MOUNTAIN

Words and Music by
MARTY ROBBINS

Slowly, with feeling

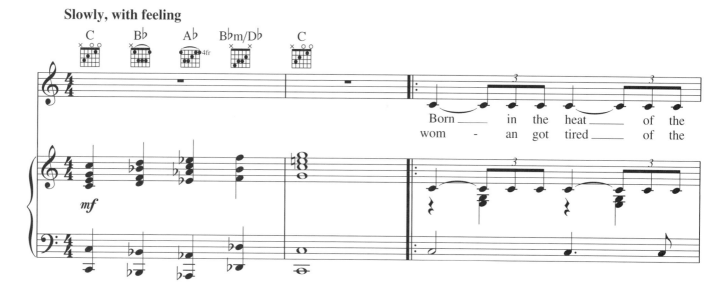

Born _____ in the heat _____ of the
wom - an got tired _____ of the

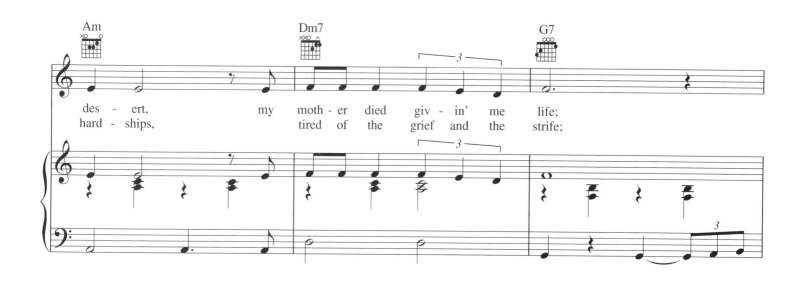

des - ert, my moth - er died giv - in' me life;
hard - ships, tired of the grief and the strife;

de - prived of the love _____ of a fa - ther, blamed _____ for the loss _____ of his
so tired _ of work - in' for noth - in', tired _____ of be - in' my

gave me a _____ moun - tain this

time. My

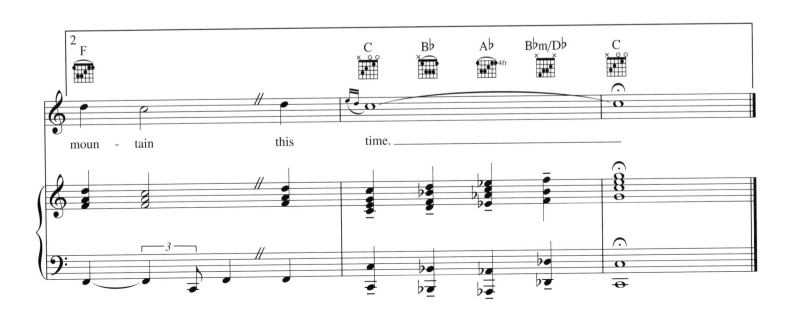

moun - tain this time. _____

THAT'S ALL RIGHT

Words and Music by
ARTHUR CRUDUP

Moderate Blues

Well, that's all right, _____ ma - ma,
ma - ma, she done told me,
leav - in' town to - mor - row,
ought - a mind my pa - pa;

that's all right for you.
pa - pa done told me too,
leav - in' town for sure;
guess I'm not too smart.

That's all right, _____
"Son, all that gal you're
then you won't be
If I was I'd

ma - ma, just _____ an - y way you do. That's all
fool - in' with, she ain't no good for you," but that's all
both - ered with me hang - in' 'round your door, but that's all
leave you, go be - fore you break my heart, but that's all

YOU'VE LOST THAT LOVIN' FEELIN'

Words and Music by BARRY MANN,
CYNTHIA WEIL and PHIL SPECTOR

MYSTERY TRAIN

Words and Music by SAM C. PHILLIPS
and HERMAN PARKER JR.

Moderately fast

1. Train I ride _____ six - teen _____
2.,3. *(See additional lyrics)*

coach - es long. _____

Train I ride _____ six - teen _____

Additional lyrics

2. Train, train, coming 'round 'round the bend.
Train, train, coming 'round 'round the bend.
Well, it took my baby, well, it never will again
(no not again.)

3. Train, train, coming down the line.
Train, train, coming down the line.
Well, it's bringing my baby 'cause she's mine, all mine
(she's mine, all mine.)

JUST PRETEND

Words and Music by GUY FLETCHER
and DOUG FLETT

ARE YOU LONESOME TONIGHT?

Words and Music by ROY TURK
and LOU HANDMAN

Are you lone-some to-night, do you miss me to-night, are you sor-ry we drift-ed a-part? _____ Does your mem-o-ry stray to a bright sum-mer day, when I kissed you and called you sweet-

WALK A MILE IN MY SHOES

Words and Music by
JOE SOUND

crit - i - cize and ac - cuse, walk a mile __ in my shoes. __

2. Now your whole ___
3. And yet we
4. There are

Additional lyrics

2. Now your whole world you see around you is just a reflection
   And the law of karma says you reap just what you sow.
   So unless you've lived a life of total perfection
   You'd better be careful of every stone that you should throw.
   Chorus

3. And yet we spend the day throwing stones at one another
   'Cause I don't think or wear my hair the same way you do.
   Well I may be common people but I'm your brother
   And when you strike out and try to hurt me it's a-hurtin' you.
   Chorus

4. There are people on reservations and out in the ghettos
   And, brother, there but for the grace of God go you and I.
   If I only had the wings of a little angel
   Don't you know I'd fly to the top of the mountain and then I'd cry.
   (*Chorus*

IN THE GHETTO
(The Vicious Circle)

Words and Music by
MAC DAVIS

To Coda

Then one night, in des - per - a - tion, the young man ___ breaks a - way. ___ He

POLK SALAD ANNIE

Words and Music by
TONY JOE WHITE

RECITATION

(Spoken:) *If some of y'all never been down south too much,*
I'm gonna tell you a little bit about this so that you'll
Understand what I'm talkin' about ...
Down there we have a plant that grows out in the woods,
And in the fields ... looks somethin' like a turnip green,
And everybody calls it polk salad, polk salad;
Used to know a girl lived down there and she'd go out
In the evenings and pick her a mess of it, carry it
Home and cook it for supper, 'cause that's about all they
Had to eat, but they did all right.

1. Down in Lou'-si-an-a where the al-li-ga-tors grow so
2. Ev-ery day 'fore sup-per-time, she'd go down by the
3. *(See additional lyrics)*

mean, there lived a girl that I swear to the world
truck patch, and pick her a mess o' polk sal-ad and

Additional Lyrics

3. Her Daddy was lazy and no count, claimed he had a bad back;
   All her brothers were fit for was stealin' watermelons out of my truck patch;
   Polk Salad Annie, the gators got your granny.
   Everybody said it was shame,
   'Cause her mama was a-workin' on the chain gang.
   (Sock a little polk salad to me, you know I need me a mess of it.)

BRIDGE OVER TROUBLED WATER

Words and Music by
PAUL SIMON

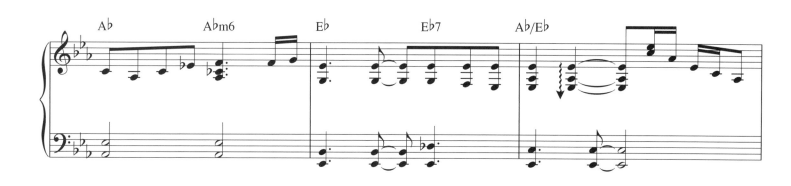

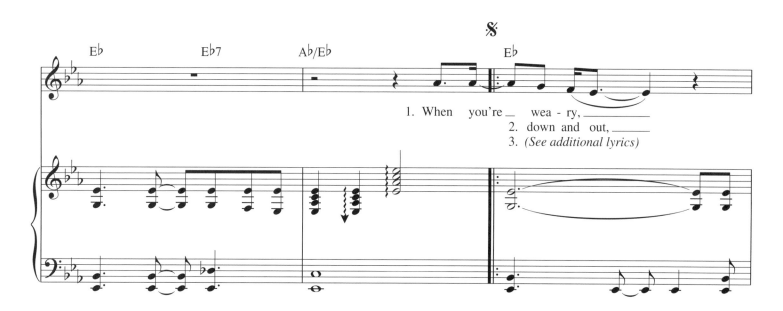

1. When you're __ wea-ry, _____
2. down and out, _____
3. *(See additional lyrics)*

When you're _

I will lay me down. _____

D.S. al Coda

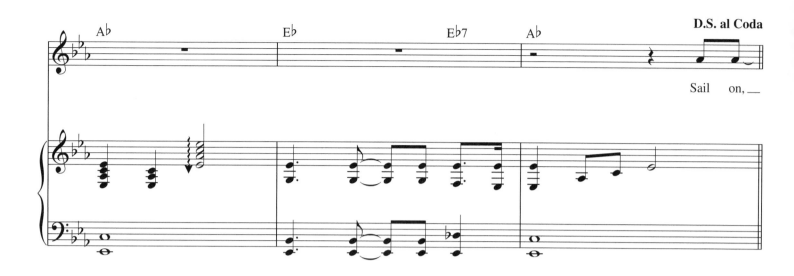

Sail on, __

CODA

trou-bled   wa - ter,   I will ease   your mind. _   Like a

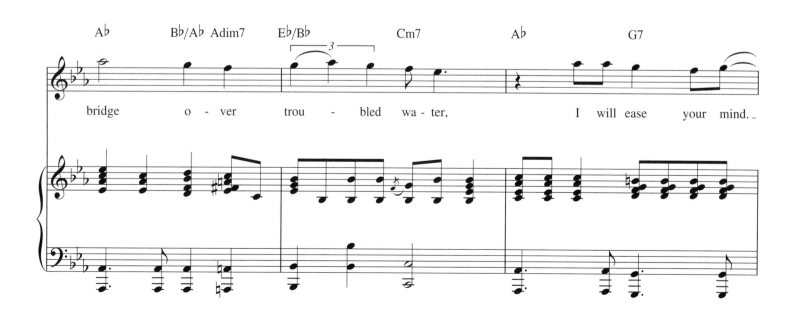

bridge   o - ver   trou - bled wa - ter,   I   will ease   your   mind. _

Additional Lyrics

3. Sail on, silver girl, sail on by.
   Your time has come to shine,
   All your dreams are on their way.
   See how they shine.
   Oh, if you need a friend,
   I'm sailing right behind.
   Chorus

THE WONDER OF YOU

Words and Music by
BAKER KNIGHT

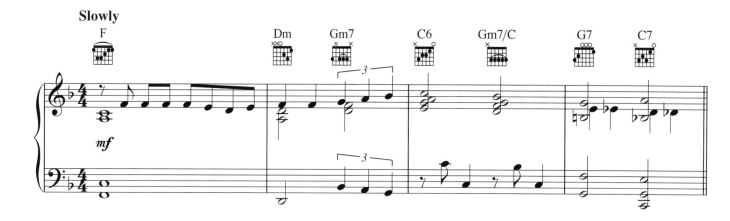

When no one else can un-der-stand me,
And when you smile, the world is bright- er.
You'll nev- er know how much I love you.

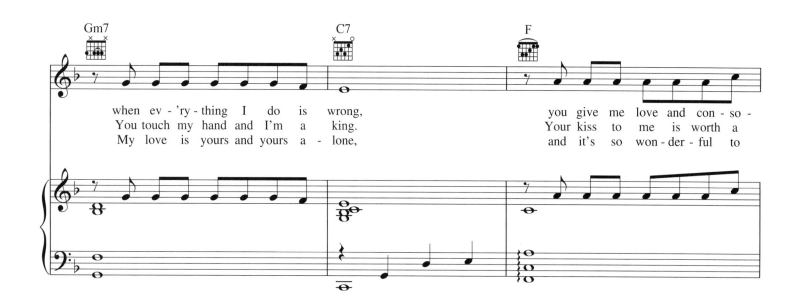

when ev-'ry-thing I do is wrong,
You touch my hand and I'm a king.
My love is yours and yours a - lone,

you give me love and con-so -
Your kiss to me is worth a
and it's so won-der-ful to

SUSPICIOUS MINDS

Words and Music by
FRANCIS ZAMBON

and we can't build our dreams

on sus - pi - cious minds. minds.

Oh, let our love sur - vive, or drive the

tears from your eyes. Let's don't let a

A BIG HUNK O' LOVE

Words and Music by AARON SCHROEDER
and SID WYCHE

MY WAY

English Words by PAUL ANKA
Original French Words by GILLES THIBAULT
Music by JACQUES REVAUX and CLAUDE FRANCOIS

HOW GREAT THOU ART

Words and Music by
STUART K. HINE

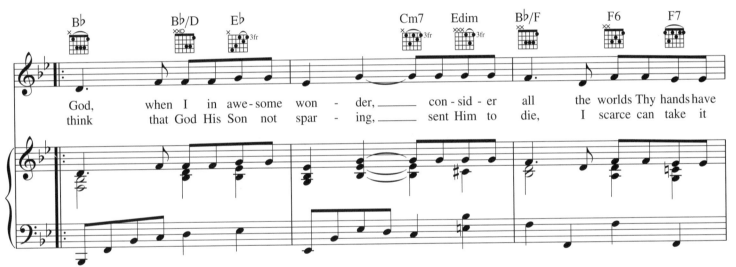

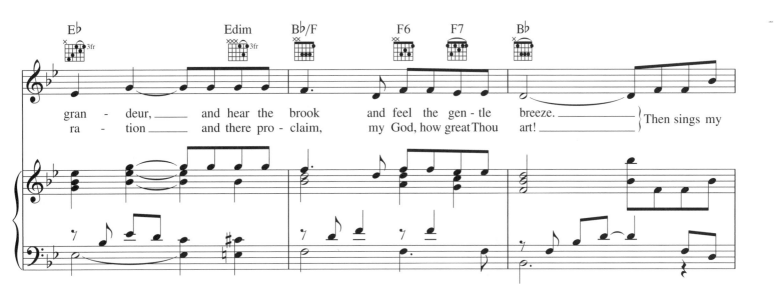

art, _____ how great Thou art! _____ Then sings my soul, my Sav-iour God to

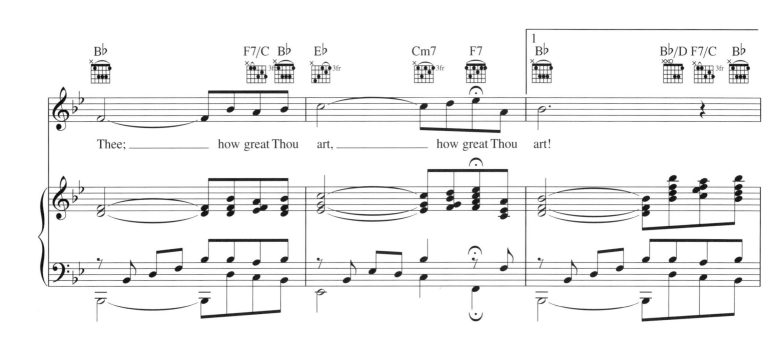

Thee; _____ how great Thou art, _____ how great Thou art!

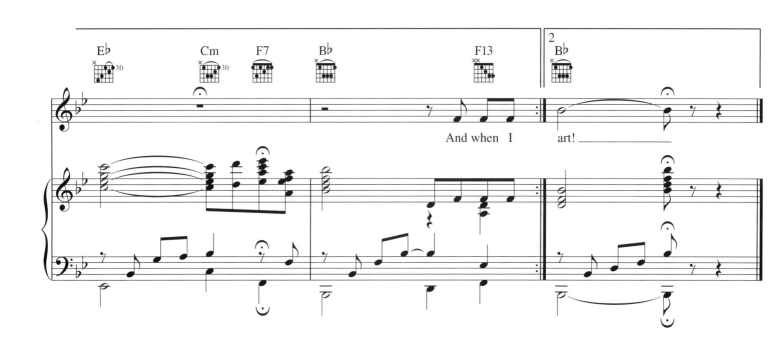

And when I art! _____

IF I CAN DREAM

Words and Music by
W. EARL BROWN

AN AMERICAN TRILOGY

Words and Music by
MICKEY NEWBURY

Moderately slow

How I wish I was in the land of cot-ton, old things they are

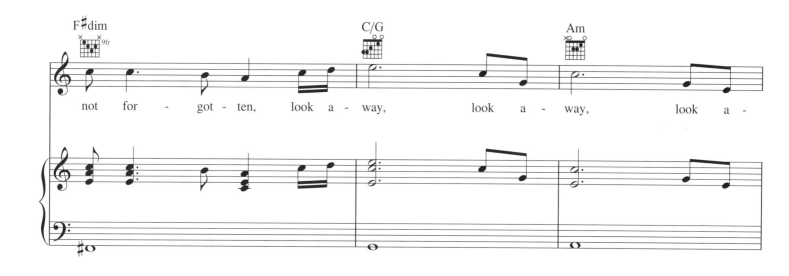

not for-got-ten, look a-way, look a-way, look a-

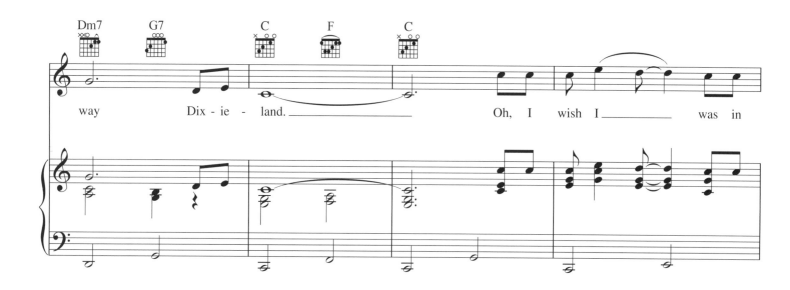

way Dix-ie-land. _____ Oh, I wish I _____ was in

CAN'T HELP FALLING IN LOVE

from the Paramount Picture BLUE HAWAII

Words and Music by GEORGE DAVID WEISS,
HUGO PERETTI and LUIGI CREATORE

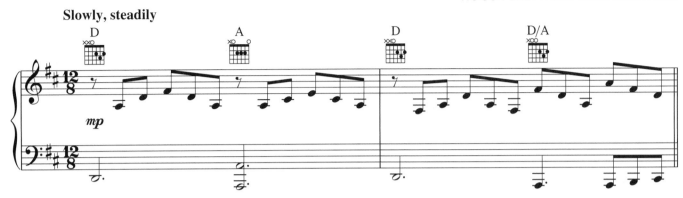

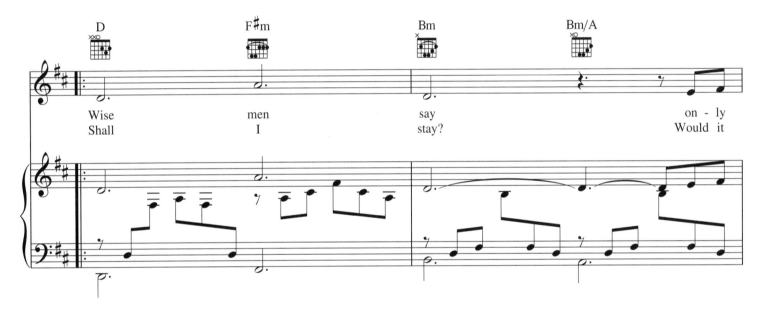

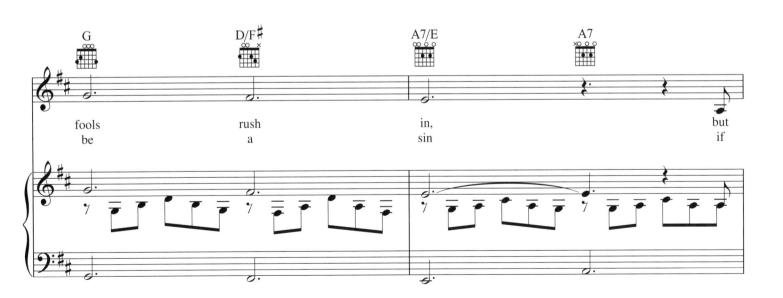